RODGERS AND HAMMERSTEIN™

VOCAL SELECTIONS

REVISED EDITION

W9-APF-509

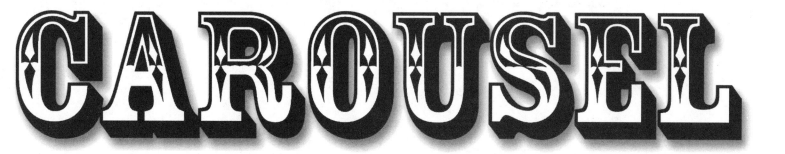

CAROUSEL

Music by
Richard Rodgers

Book and Lyrics by
Oscar Hammerstein II

Based on Ferenc Molnar's play "Liliom"
As adapted by Benjamin F. Glazer

Cover Photo by Joan Marcus
(Sally Murphy and Michael Hayden from the 1994 Broadway Production of CAROUSEL)

ISBN 0-88188-636-X

WILLIAMSON MUSIC®
A RODGERS AND HAMMERSTEIN COMPANY
www.williamsonmusic.com

EXCLUSIVELY DISTRIBUTED BY

HAL•LEONARD®
CORPORATION
7777 W. BLUEMOUND RD. P.O. BOX 13819 MILWAUKEE, WI 53213

Visit Hal Leonard Online at
www.halleonard.com

Rodgers and Hammerstein's

CAROUSEL

"AS CLOSE TO PERFECTION AS MUSICAL THEATRE GETS!"
— *The Boston Globe*

To learn more about CAROUSEL and the other great musicals
available for production through R&H Theatricals,
please visit our website
www.rnhtheatricals.com
or contact

229 W. 28TH ST., 11th FLOOR
NEW YORK, NEW YORK 10001

THEATRICALS

PHONE: (212)564-4000
FAX: (212)268-1245
E-MAIL: theatre@rnh.com

All photos (unless otherwise noted) provided courtesy of
The Rodgers & Hammerstein Organization

CAROUSEL

CONTENTS

The authors celebrate two of their Broadway runs in the mid 1940s.

Jan Clayton as Julie Jordan and John Raitt as Billy Bigelow

RICHARD RODGERS & OSCAR HAMMERSTEIN II

After long and highly distinguished careers with other collaborators, Richard Rodgers (composer) and Oscar Hammerstein II (librettist/lyricist) joined forces to create the most consistently fruitful and successful partnership in the American musical theatre.

Prior to his work with Hammerstein, Richard Rodgers (1902-1979) collaborated with lyricist Lorenz Hart on a series of musical comedies that epitomized the wit and sophistication of Broadway in its heyday. Prolific on Broadway, in London and in Hollywood from the '20s into the early '40s, Rodgers & Hart wrote more than forty shows and film scores. Among their greatest were ON YOUR TOES, BABES IN ARMS, THE BOYS FROM SYRACUSE, I MARRIED AN ANGEL and PAL JOEY.

Throughout the same era Oscar Hammerstein II (1895-1960) brought new life to a moribund artform: the operetta. His collaborations with such preeminent composers as Rudolf Friml, Sigmund Romberg and Vincent Youmans resulted in such operetta classics as THE DESERT SONG, ROSE-MARIE and THE NEW MOON. With Jerome Kern he wrote SHOW BOAT, the 1927 masterpiece that changed the course of modern musical theatre. His last musical before embarking on an exclusive partnership with Richard Rodgers was CARMEN JONES, the highly-acclaimed 1943 all-black revision of Georges Bizet's tragic opera CARMEN.

OKLAHOMA!, the first Rodgers & Hammerstein musical, was also the first of a new genre, the musical play, representing a unique fusion of Rodgers' musical comedy and Hammerstein's operetta. A milestone in the development of the American musical, it also marked the beginning of the most successful partnership in Broadway musical history, and was followed by CAROUSEL, ALLEGRO, SOUTH PACIFIC, THE KING AND I, ME AND JULIET, PIPE DREAM, FLOWER DRUM SONG and THE SOUND OF MUSIC. Rodgers & Hammerstein wrote one musical specifically for the big screen, STATE FAIR, and one for television, CINDERELLA. Collectively, the Rodgers & Hammerstein musicals earned 35 Tony

United States postage stamp honoring Rodgers and Hammerstein, issued September 21, 1999.

Awards, 15 Academy Awards, two Pulitzer Prizes, two Grammy Awards and two Emmy Awards. In 1998 Rodgers & Hammerstein were cited by *Time* Magazine and CBS News as among the 20 most influential artists of the 20th century, and in 1999 they were jointly commemorated on a U.S. postage stamp.

Despite Hammerstein's death in 1960, Rodgers continued to write for the Broadway stage. His first solo entry, NO STRINGS, earned him two Tony Awards for music and lyrics, and was followed by DO I HEAR A WALTZ?, TWO BY TWO, REX and I REMEMBER MAMA. Richard Rodgers died on December 30, 1979, less than eight months after his last musical opened on Broadway. In March of 1990, Broadway's 46th Street Theatre was renamed The Richard Rodgers Theatre in his honor.

At the turn of the 21st century, the Rodgers and Hammerstein legacy continued to flourish, as marked by the enthusiasm that greeted their Centennials in 1995 and 2002.

In 1995, Hammerstein's centennial was celebrated worldwide with commemorative recordings, books, concerts and an award-winning PBS special, "Some Enchanted Evening." The ultimate tribute came the following season, when he had three musicals playing on Broadway simultaneously: SHOW BOAT (1995 Tony Award winner, Best Musical Revival); THE KING AND I (1996 Tony Award winner, Best Musical Revival); and STATE FAIR (1996 Tony Award nominee for Best Score).

In 2002, the Richard Rodgers Centennial was celebrated around the world, with tributes from Tokyo to London, from the Hollywood Bowl to the White House, featuring six new television specials, museum retrospectives, a dozen new ballets, half a dozen books, new recordings and countless concert and stage productions (including three simultaneous revivals on Broadway, matching Hammerstein's feat of six years earlier), giving testament to the enduring popularity of Richard Rodgers and the sound of his music.

SOMETHING GOOD
A Broadway Salute to Richard Rodgers on His 100th Birthday

Friday, June 28, 2002
Gershwin Theatre • New York City

Something Wonderful

A Celebration of Oscar Hammerstein II
on his 100th birthday

Wednesday, July 12, 1995
New York

SYNOPSIS

The time is 1873. The place, a small fishing village on the rocky New England coastline. Billy Bigelow, the handsome and swaggering barker for Mrs. Mullin's carousel in the local amusement park, meets Julie Jordan, a lovely young girl working at the nearby mill, when Julie and her friend Carrie Pipperidge come to the carousel (**"The Carousel Waltz"**).

Billy has taken up with Jigger Craigin, a shifty fellow off one of the whaling ships. Jigger has come to town with a couple of his pals, looking for trouble—and more (**"Blow High, Blow Low"**). He seeks to persuade Billy to join him in a robbery scheme. Billy resists—until Julie quietly gives Billy some important news: she is going to have a child. Billy will do anything to help his child—anything (**"Soliloquy"**).

Carousel barker Billy Bigelow (John Raitt, on pedestal, left) lures customers at the fairground in the Prelude.

The townsfolk are enjoying themselves at a beachside feast (**"A Real Nice Clambake"**). Jigger indulges in some not-so-harmless flirting with Carrie, which upsets her Mr. Snow and his plan for happy domesticity (**"Geraniums in the Winder"**).

Later, while the clambake continues, Billy and Jigger slip off to the pier to commit their robbery. With Billy gone, the women gather around Julie, their intuition telling them that she is desperately unhappy. She is. But she is also in love (**"What's the Use of Wond'rin'"**).

As Carrie Pipperidge (Jean Darling) sings of her future husband to her friends, Mr. Snow himself (Eric Mattson) looks on.

This was "A Real Nice Clambake." The opening number from Act II.

A short time later, Carrie is telling Julie about her new beau (**"Mister Snow"**) when Billy arrives. Though Carrie runs off, Julie stays behind. Billy and Julie are irresistibly drawn to each other (**"If I Loved You"**).

Months later, the villagers are celebrating the end of a long winter and the start of a glorious summer (**"June Is Bustin' Out All Over"**). Julie and Billy are married, but there is trouble. Billy is out of work, and has treated Julie badly. Carrie wishes that Julie's husband could be more like her chivalrous Mr. Snow, who woos Carrie with his picture of what wedded life will be like for them (**"When the Children Are Asleep"**).

Photos from the original 1945 Broadway production

As the townspeople look on in horror, Billy Bigelow (John Raitt) lays dying in a climactic scene from Act II.

Meanwhile, back at the dock, the burglary attempt is thwarted; Jigger escapes, but Billy is caught by Mr. Bascombe, the would-be victim, who vows to hand him over to the police with the prospect of a long prison term. Cornered, disgraced and terrified for Julie and their unborn child, Billy stabs himself. Julie arrives on the scene and cradles Billy as he dies in her arms. Julie is distraught, but wise Nettie Fowler offers her comfort (**"You'll Never Walk Alone"**).

Fifteen years pass. Billy, escorted by a Heavenly Friend, arrives in the backyard of Heaven (**"The Highest Judge of All"**). Here he meets the Starkeeper, who informs him that he will never get into Heaven until he redeems himself. After some argument, Billy is given a chance. He is allowed to return to Earth for one day, during which he must perform one good deed. Afforded a glimpse of Louise, his lonely and unhappy fifteen-year-old daughter, Billy steals a star to give to her at their first meeting. But back on earth, he is still the rough blunderer. Louise is shy and won't accept his gift. Frustrated, unable to reach her in any other way, Billy slaps his daughter—but the sting feels miraculously like a kiss to the girl. Louise explains this to her mother, Julie, who also sees the star that Billy has left behind. Julie instinctively understands.

Nevertheless, Billy has not yet performed his good deed, and the slap should have been the final straw. But Billy persuades the Starkeeper to give him one last chance. Unseen, Billy watches Louise at her high school graduation. He observes his daughter's self-doubts and her insecurities. Invisibly, spiritually, Billy reaches out to her; he urges her to believe in herself, and he is filled with pride as he watches his daughter blossom with confidence. Turning to Julie, Billy says simply, "I loved you, Julie. Know that I loved you." And Julie, somehow, hears him. She joins Louise and the rest of the townsfolk in singing "You'll Never Walk Alone"... as Billy heads toward his redemption.

Louise (Bambi Linn) is apprehensive when a stranger—whom she does not know is her deceased father, Billy Bigelow (John Raitt)—tries to present her with a Heavenly Star.

TURNS ON THE *CAROUSEL*

OKLAHOMA!, the first musical Rodgers & Hammerstein wrote together, wasn't a mere success: it was a phenomenon. An artistic triumph that changed the course of musical theatre, it shattered box office records when it opened in 1943, outran every show before it, held Broadway's longevity crown for fifteen years, and launched the Rodgers & Hammerstein partnership as Broadway's Golden Team in Broadway's Golden Era.

Inevitably the question arose: what could possibly follow OKLAHOMA!? In his autobiography Rodgers recalls the sage advice he received from film mogul Sam Goldwyn: "This is such a wonderful show!" Goldwyn bubbled. "You know what you should do next? Shoot yourself!"

Fortunately, Rodgers & Hammerstein had other ideas in mind. Their first assignment after OKLAHOMA! was a new work in another medium altogether— writing the score for a movie musical called STATE FAIR (1945), a charming depiction of homespun Americana that introduced "It Might As Well Be Spring," the Academy Award winner for Best Song of the Year.

Still, Hollywood was only a detour on the return to Broadway. As with OKLAHOMA!, it was Rodgers & Hammerstein's producers, Lawrence Langner and Theresa Helburn of The Theatre Guild, who provided the team with the source for their next musical. In two previous, successful instances, Helburn and Langner had recycled Guild plays into Guild musicals (turning PORGY into PORGY AND BESS, and GREEN GROW THE LILACS into OKLAHOMA!). Now, the Guild wanted Rodgers & Hammerstein to make a musical out of LILIOM.

Hungarian playwright Ferenc Molnar's elaborate fantasy had its American premiere under the auspices of The Theatre Guild, in a 1921 production translated by Benjamin F. Glazer that starred Joseph Schildkraut in the title role and Eva Le Gallienne as Julie. The property was rich with musical potential, but before it could be transformed Helburn and Langner had to convince not only their skeptical American authors, but also their Hungarian one.

THE THEATRE GUILD presents

Carousel

A New Musical Play

Based on FERENC MOLNAR'S "LILIOM" as adapted by Benjamin F. Glazer

Music by RICHARD RODGERS
Book and Lyrics by OSCAR HAMMERSTEIN 2d
Directed by ROUBEN MAMOULIAN
Dances by AGNES DE MILLE
Settings by JO MIELZINER
Costumes by MILES WHITE

with
JOHN RAITT · JAN CLAYTON
Christine Johnson · Eric Mattson · Jean Casto
and a Bright Young Cast of Singers and Dancers

PRODUCTION SUPERVISED BY LAWRENCE LANGNER AND THERESA HELBURN

COLONIAL THEATRE
BOSTON

3 Weeks Only, Beg. Tues., March 27

MATINEES THURSDAY & SATURDAY
PRICES: Eves. $1.20, $2.40, $3.00, $3.60, $4.20.
Sat. Mat. $1.20, $1.80, $2.40, $3.00, $3.60.
Thurs. Mat. $1.20, $1.80, $2.40, $3.00.

Poster for the Pre-Broadway Boston run

Molnar had already turned down several requests to turn LILIOM into an opera. And he was ready to resist again, until, at the Guild's invitation, he attended a performance of OKLAHOMA! and was instantly won over. LILIOM could sing, he decreed, if Rodgers & Hammerstein wrote the score.

But Rodgers & Hammerstein had their doubts too. It was not the themes of domestic violence and fateful tragedy in LILIOM that deterred the authors—in fact, these issues only served to whet their appetite for challenging work—but the play's locale: Budapest, Hungary. In 1944 Budapest was ravaged by war, and setting a play there would only compete with the headlines, or worse, seem exploitive.

If a musical of LILIOM were to work, they concluded, it would have to be relocated, and Rodgers and Hammerstein were reluctant to do so. Helburn suggested a New Orleans setting, with Liliom turned into a tough and exotic Creole character. Oscar Hammerstein demurred on the grounds that his lyrics, which were always steeped in the dialect of their locale, would become riddled with the "ze's" and "zose's" of the Creole accent and end up sounding like a chorus of buzz saws.

But then Richard Rodgers came up with the concept of New England in the late 19th century and everything fell into place. Liliom would become Billy Bigelow, barker on a carousel in a small fishing village, and Julie would be featured as one of the local millworkers. While images of clambakes and lighthouses danced in their heads, the authors went to work. The very first song they wrote for the score was the most daunting— Billy's powerful and insightful "Soliloquy." As daring as anything in the groundbreaking OKLAHOMA!, this number provided character, motivation, passion and heartfelt emotion—in an unprecedented eight-minute solo.

Structurally, CAROUSEL proved as daring as OKLAHOMA! in style and form, while telling a story that was far more sophisticated. Here, in addition to Billy's "Soliloquy," the innovations included the opening, which scuttled the traditional overture entirely and replaced it with a lush "Carousel Waltz" that underscored a storied prologue in mime; and the now-classic "If I Loved You" scene, in which dialogue and fragments of song were intermingled to breathtaking effects.

Julie (Jan Clayton) comforts her daughter Louise (Bambi Linn).

n Clayton as Julie Jordan and hn Raitt as Billy Bigelow

CAROUSEL began rehearsals in early 1945. Guiding it was OKLAHOMA!'s stellar creative team: authors Rodgers & Hammerstein, producers Helburn and Langner, director Rouben Mamoulian, choreographer Agnes de Mille and costume designer Miles White. Featured in the original cast were John Raitt as Billy, Jan Clayton as Julie Jordan, and Jean Darling as Carrie.

After tryouts in New Haven and Boston, CAROUSEL opened at Broadway's Majestic Theatre on April 19, 1945, and eventually ran for 890 performances. Even the skeptics were confounded: while it could never be the unexpected revelation that OKLAHOMA! was, CAROUSEL did the impossible—it followed a smash hit by succeeding in its own right. Audiences in the throes of World War II responded deeply to its story of a young widow raising a child alone, and its spiritual imagery had a profound impact on those who had lost a loved one overseas. The effects of CAROUSEL and its anthem, "You'll Never Walk Alone," are haunting to this day.

Winner of the New York Drama Critics' Circle Award as Best Musical of 1945, the Broadway run was followed by a two-year national tour. In London, CAROUSEL followed OKLAHOMA! directly into the Theatre Royal, Drury Lane, opening in June of 1950 and playing for over a year and a half. In 1956 the motion picture version was released by Twentieth Century Fox. Filmed on location in Boothbay Harbor, Maine, it was originally slated to star Frank Sinatra as Billy and Judy Garland as Julie. However, she withdrew prior to filming and he left over a contract dispute during the first weeks of shooting. They were replaced by the OKLAHOMA! movie co-stars Gordon MacRae and Shirley Jones.

To date, CAROUSEL has been performed by hundreds of theatre and opera companies throughout the world; R&H Theatricals licenses an average of 300 productions of CAROUSEL a year in the United States alone. Notable productions include the Music Theater of Lincoln Center, with John Raitt re-creating the role of Billy (1965); a television version starring Robert Goulet with choreography by Edward Villella, broadcast on ABC-TV (1967); and a summer run at the U.S. Pavilion of the 1958 Brussels Exposition, with Jan Clayton re-creating the role of Julie. By the late 20th Century, opera companies began performing CAROUSEL as well, including Lyric Opera of Chicago and Houston Grand Opera.

Original sheet music cover

In 1992, director Nicholas Hytner, choreographer Sir Kenneth MacMillan and designer Bob Crowley collaborated on the revelatory Royal National Theatre production of CAROUSEL in London, which played to sold-out houses in the Lyttleton Theatre before transferring to the Shaftesbury Theatre in the West End the following September, where it was presented by Cameron Mackintosh.

That production transferred to New York in March of 1994, marking the musical's first return to Broadway since the original run. It ran for a year at the Vivian Beaumont Theater, presented by Lincoln Center Theater, where it went on to receive a record-setting five Tony Awards (the most of any show that season), including Best Musical Revival. A Japanese production played extended engagements in Tokyo, Nagoya and Osaka in 1995, and a U.S. National Tour visited over 40 cities from February of 1996 through May of 1997.

Yet another turn on the CAROUSEL yielded two more brass rings in 2002. Then, during the Centennial celebrations for Richard Rodgers, his personal favorite of his musicals was performed in two unforgettable and stellar concert performances—first at New York's Carnegie Hall and then at London's Royal Festival Hall. The June 6th concert at Carnegie Hall starred Hugh Jackman in his New York stage debut as Billy, and Audra McDonald as Julie. (McDonald had won her

first Tony for playing Carrie in the 1994 Broadway revival), with Leonard Slatkin conducting the Orchestra of St. Luke's. The June 15th concert in London starred Spencer McLaren as Billy and Emily Loesser as Julie, with David Charles Abell conducting the BBC Concert Orchestra. As memorable as the London event was, the New York concert had one extra moment that surpassed everything else: a surprise cameo appearance on the stage of Carnegie Hall from original CAROUSEL star John Raitt. He received a standing ovation from the crowd, and an embrace from Hugh Jackman; it was to be Mr. Raitt's final appearance on a New York stage.

Robert Pagent and Bambi Linn dance a sensuous pas de deux from the Act II ballet, choreographed by Agnes de Mille.

Julie (Jan Clayton, far right) senses the presence of her deceased husband Billy Bigelow (John Raitt) during the emotional finale of CAROUSEL.

Jan Clayton as Julie Jordan and John Raitt as Billy Bigelow

BLOW HIGH, BLOW LOW

Lyrics by OSCAR HAMMERSTEIN II

Music by RICHARD RODGERS

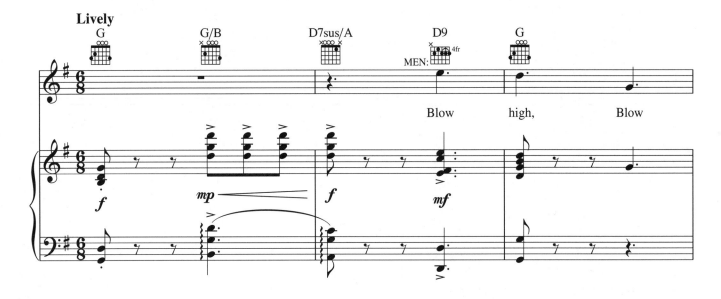

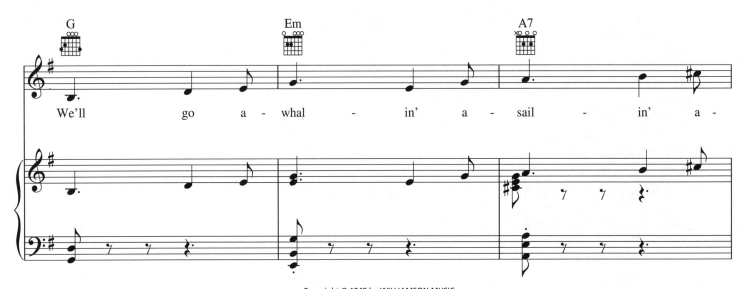

The
It's
A

peo - ple who live on land ____ Are hard to un - der -
won - der - ful just to feel ____ Your hands up - on a
rock - in' up - on the sea, ____ Your boat will seem to

stand, ____ When you're look - in' for fun, They clap you in - to
wheel, ____ And to lis - ten to wind a - whist - lin' in a
be ____ Like a dear lit - tle ba - by in her bas - sin -

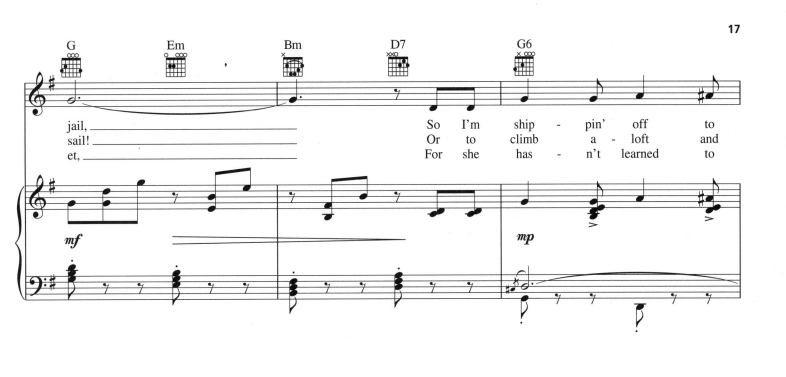

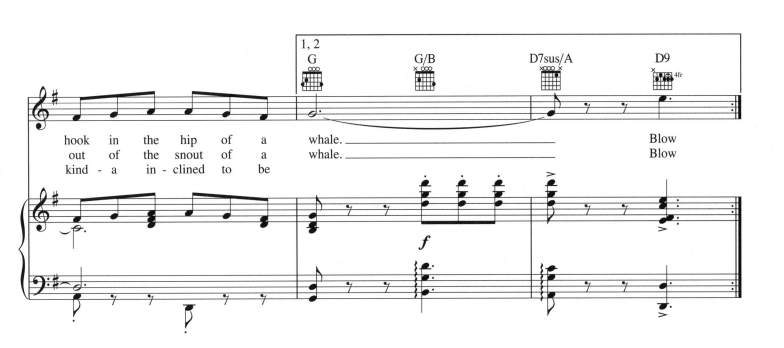

D.S. al Coda

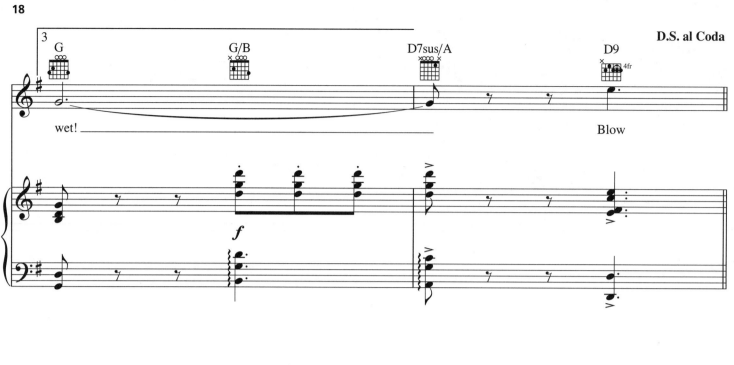

wet! _____ Blow

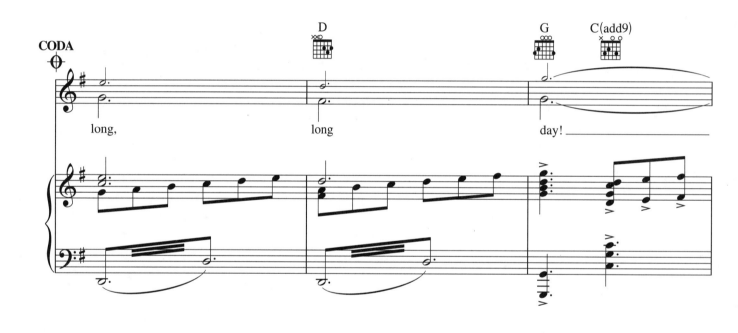

long,   long   day! _____

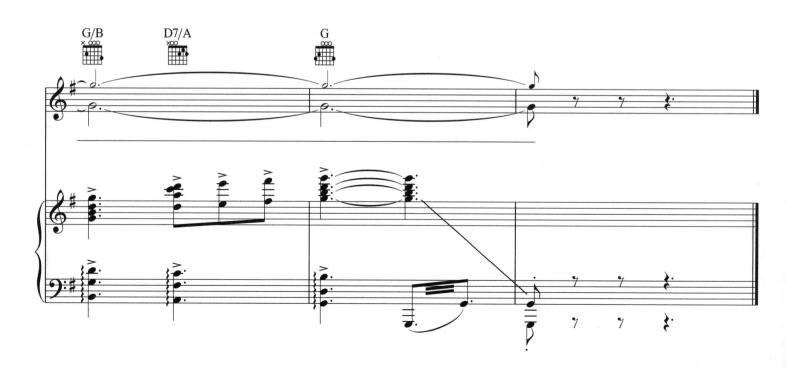

GERANIUMS IN THE WINDER

Lyrics by OSCAR HAMMERSTEIN II

Music by RICHARD RODGERS

THE CAROUSEL WALTZ

Music by RICHARD RODGERS

Allegro moderato

p dolce

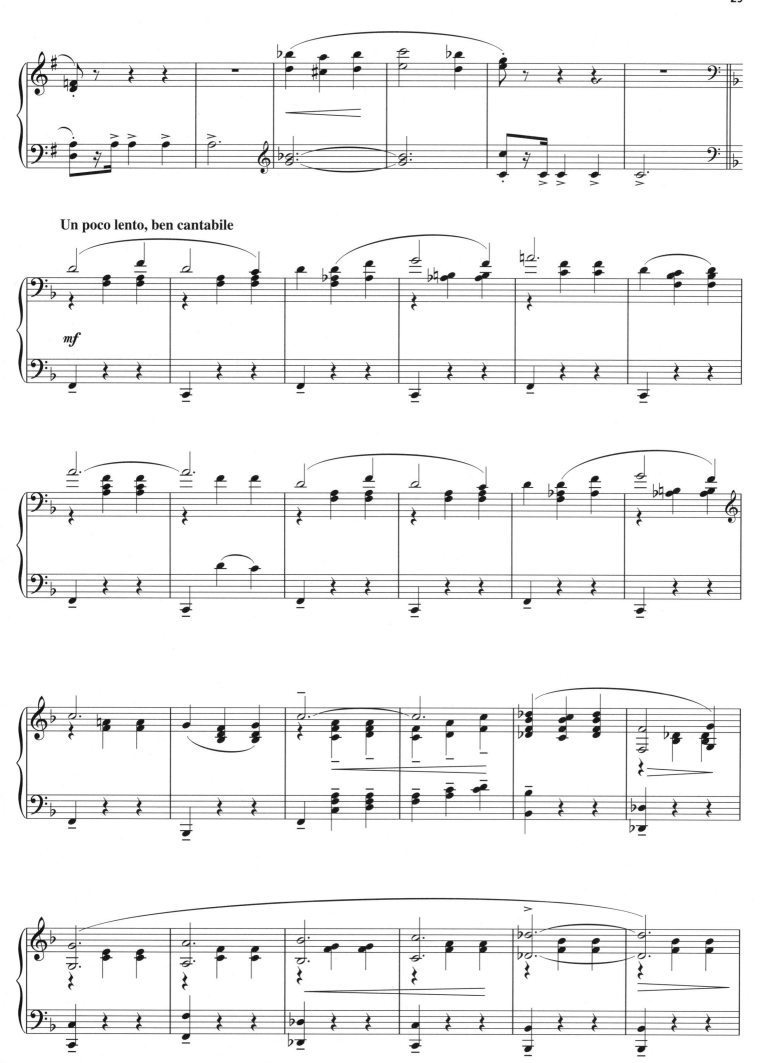

Un poco lento, ben cantabile

THE HIGHEST JUDGE OF ALL

Lyrics by OSCAR HAMMERSTEIN II

Music by RICHARD RODGERS

hear my doom! Take me be-yond the pearl-y gates, Through a beau-ti-ful mar-ble

mf a tempo

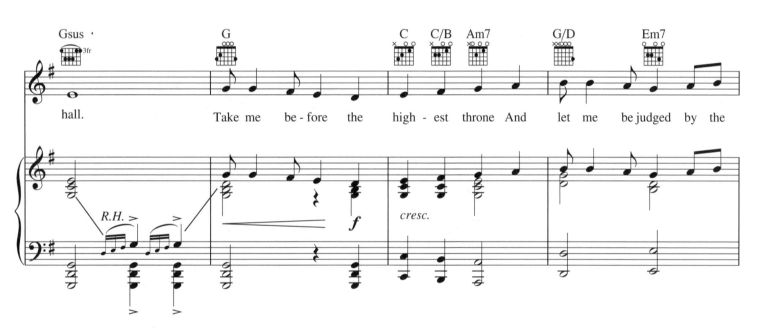

hall. Take me be-fore the high-est throne And let me be judged by the

R.H. *f* *cresc.*

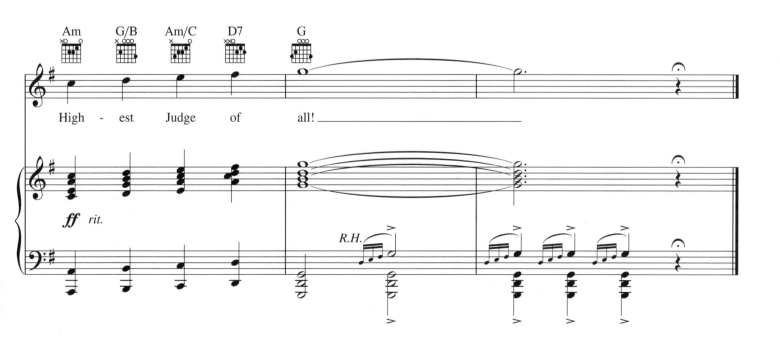

High-est Judge of all! _____

ff *rit.*

R.H.

IF I LOVED YOU

Lyrics by OSCAR HAMMERSTEIN II

Music by RICHARD RODGERS

JUNE IS BUSTIN' OUT ALL OVER

Lyrics by OSCAR HAMMERSTEIN II

Music by RICHARD RODGERS

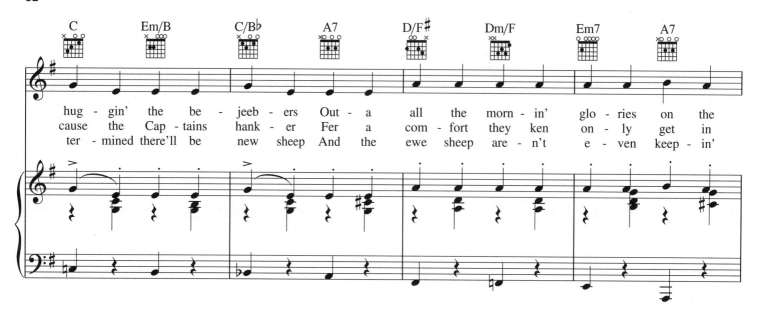

hug - gin' the be - jeeb - ers Out - a all the morn - in' glo - ries on the
cause the Cap - tains hank - er Fer a com - fort they ken on - ly get in
ter - mined there'll be new sheep And the ewe sheep are - n't e - ven keep - in'

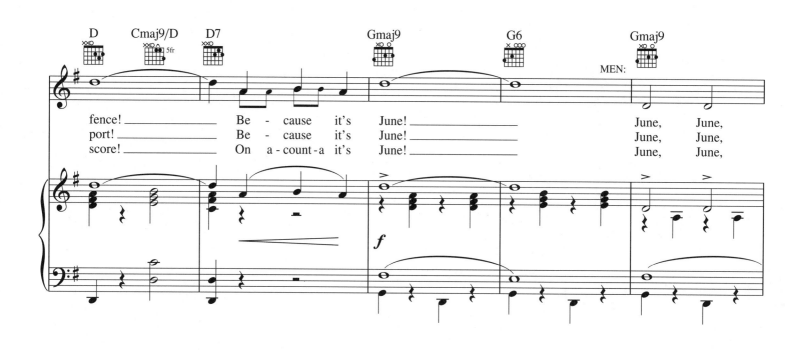

fence! _____ Be - cause it's June! _____ June, June,
port! _____ Be - cause it's June! _____ June, June,
score! _____ On a - count - a it's June! _____ June, June,

MEN:

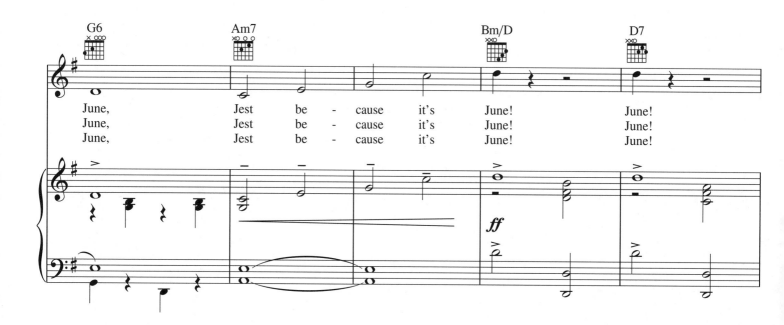

June, Jest be - cause it's June! June!
June, Jest be - cause it's June! June!
June, Jest be - cause it's June! June!

MISTER SNOW

Lyrics by OSCAR HAMMERSTEIN II

Music by RICHARD RODGERS

Refrain, Moderato *(with expression)*

When I mar - ry Mis - ter Snow,

The flow - ers 'll be buzz - in' with the hum of bees, The

birds 'll make a rack - et in the church - yard trees, When I mar - ry Mis - ter

Snow. Then it's off to home we'll

60

A REAL NICE CLAMBAKE

Lyrics by OSCAR HAMMERSTEIN II

Music by RICHARD RODGERS

pop-pin' from their shells, Jest how man-y of them gal-loped down our gul-lets.

Subito allegro

We could-n't say our-sel's oh _____ h _____

h! This was a real nice clam-bake, _____

_____ We're might-y glad we came, _____

SOLILOQUY

Lyrics by OSCAR HAMMERSTEIN II

Music by RICHARD RODGERS

Broader *(with warmth)*

(Spoken:) I can just hear myself bragging about her!

My lit- tle girl, Pink and white As peach- es and cream is she. My lit- tle girl Is half a- gain as bright As girls are meant to be! Doz- ens of boys pur- sue her, Man- y a like- ly

WHEN THE CHILDREN ARE ASLEEP

Lyrics by OSCAR HAMMERSTEIN II

Music by RICHARD RODGERS

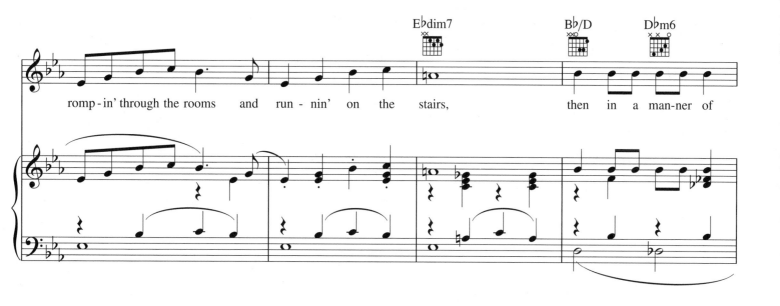

once they close their eyes, and we are left a-lone and free from all their fuss,

then in a man-ner of speak-in' we can be real-ly

us. When the chil-dren are a-sleep, we'll sit and

WHAT'S THE USE OF WOND'RIN'

Lyrics by OSCAR HAMMERSTEIN II

Music by RICHARD RODGERS

YOU'LL NEVER WALK ALONE

Lyrics by OSCAR HAMMERSTEIN II

Music by RICHARD RODGERS

* alternate lyric: hold your head up high